# The Tales Of Tears

CREATIVE RAMON MEDIA & PUBLISHING LLC
Copyright © 2018 Eric Ramon Taylor
Library of Congress Control Number: 002089270

All rights reserved. This book or any portion thereof
may not be reproduced or used in any manner whatsoever
without the express written permission of the publisher and author
except for the use of brief quotations in a book review.

Printed in the United States of America

.

ISBN-13: 978-1-7329567-0-4

www.creativeramon.com

# DEDICATION

*I dedicate this book,*
*To my son and my daughter*
*My motivation for writing,*
*When I didn't want to bother*
*My constant light,*
*Through all my storms*

*Forever burning bright,*
*And fixing what was torn*
*Finding what was lost*
*And what I was deprived of*
*Given without a cost*
*In the form of a hug*

*Your love!*

# AKNOWLEGEMENTS

I would like to express my gratitude to the many people who saw me through this book; to all those who provided support, talked things over, read, offered comments and assisted in the editing, proofreading and design. Your belief in my writings were pivotal in this books creation.

I would like to thank all those whom inspired the poems in this book, although most were created in the midst of hard times, I am grateful that something good has come out of them.

Thanks to my Uncle Sylvester Taylor, for literally believing in my writings so much that he was willing to act to create a book, when I was still uncertain - without you this book would never find its way to the public.

Thanks to my family, son, daughter and sisters. You are my motivation, the fuel that drove me to completing this book.

Last and not least: I would like to thank Pastor Venus Stafford, the first person to ever to hear and believe in my writing. She is literally the reason why I kept writing, she made the 17 year old me feel special when she first heard my prayer and it made me want to write more.

He said patience my son, your day will come
Followed by greatness like the fame of the son
So doubt me, I am God almighty
I have the world in my hands; I've been here from the start
A father and a friend, I gave this world my heart
So, if I promise success it's within your reach
Follow suit my child and hear me teach

# CONTENTS

| | |
|---|---|
| DEDICATION | iii |
| AKNOWLEGEMENTS | iv |
| PRAYER | 1 |
| Lost Success | 3 |
| Struggle Sanity | 4 |
| I Digress | 6 |
| Genesis | 8 |
| Drifters | 10 |
| Don't Cry | 12 |
| Where's My Daddy At | 14 |
| Taken | 16 |
| Thought I Was Grown | 18 |
| Change | 20 |
| My First Poem (7th Grade) | 22 |
| I'm fighting Again | 25 |
| Happy Birthday | 29 |
| Success | 31 |
| Reminiscing | 32 |
| Our Life | 34 |
| Am I a Preacher? | 36 |
| Dead World | 38 |
| Forgive Me | 40 |
| Heavenly Beauty | 41 |
| Dear John | 43 |
| Dear Jane | 44 |
| Breathe | 45 |
| Fear None | 47 |
| Rage | 49 |

| | |
|---|---|
| Progression | 51 |
| Prayer | 53 |
| Broken Spirits | 54 |
| Broken Spirit II | 56 |
| FATHER | 58 |
| FATHER II | 60 |
| No More | 62 |
| Unleashed | 64 |
| Venus Angel | 66 |
| Poverty Victim | 68 |
| Crystal Clear | 70 |
| My Intentions | 71 |
| I have to make it | 72 |
| Father Issues | 73 |
| New Year New Sorrow | 74 |
| Cursed from Birth | 75 |
| My Struggle | 76 |
| Am I still me | 77 |
| So Perfect | 78 |
| Lust | 79 |
| A Love Like | 80 |
| Happy Anniversary | 81 |
| I Remember | 82 |
| Rest in Peace | 83 |
| Emotional Scribe | 84 |
| The Thought of You | 85 |
| Under Appreciated | 86 |
| How to be a Father | 87 |
| Sleeping Demons | 88 |
| Bedtime Prayer II | 90 |

| | |
|---|---|
| Another Lost Soul | 91 |
| I'm Still Dreaming | 92 |
| A Man's Pride | 93 |
| Reliving The Past | 94 |
| Resolution | 95 |
| Hush Little Dove | 96 |
| These Tears | 97 |
| Visions | 98 |
| She Was Beautiful | 99 |
| She was there | 100 |
| Last Love | 101 |
| I Survived (The War on Cancer) | 102 |
| My Awakening | 104 |
| I'm Still Waking Up | 106 |
| I Can See | 107 |
| Consciousism (We Weren't Christians) | 108 |
| They hear but don't listen | 109 |
| Have You Ever | 111 |
| Don't look back | 113 |
| You don't know | 114 |
| Lie to me | 115 |
| Dreaming of Tomorrow | 116 |
| Tempted (But I remember) | 117 |
| Drink Up | 119 |
| The Brain vs The Heart | 120 |
| Married in the spring | 121 |
| How Much | 122 |
| I'm Sorry | 123 |
| Love is Blinding | 124 |
| There's A Place | 125 |
| Final Thoughts | 126 |

# PRAYER

Our Father, who are in heaven

Forgive us for our sins before and after eleven

The sins of men which has damned us from the ages of pharaohs and kings

For now, we know all things are possible with you on our team

And to know you, is to trust you, so we step out on our faith and dreams

And believe you, we're nothing without you, we need you

And love you, and don't doubt you, even though we can't see you

Because to know about you is to love you

So, we see what we feel and put nothing above you

So, we give thanks to you for blessing us

And know that our challenges are you testing us

So in our times of need, when we feel our lowest

We're not alone, in fact, we are at our closest

At our closest and then some, to love, but fear none

And to know the best is yet to come

Our Fathers lead us

For Your Son, His sacrifice has freed us.

~~~~~~~~~~~~~~~~~~~~~~~~~~~*****~~~~~~~~~~~~~~~~~~~~~~~~~~~

*This prayer is the first of its kind; it is the first prayer I ever wrote. The response I got from those who heard this, is one of the reasons I initially began writing. At one point, I had it as the voicemail message on my phone and there were a few incidents where people called and had the wrong number, they would leave me a message just to tell me how much they liked the prayer. So that's the reason I decided to start my first book off with this poem. It symbolizes the birth of a new found talent which has gotten me through numerous events in my life both disastrous and noteworthy. All which will be depicted on further pages as you continue to read on.*

# Lost Success

*Eric Taylor, I remember him; we never talked, but we were cool. Quiet kid, nonchalant, he was cool, real smooth.*

Foster care, poverty, you name it and I did it twice, plus one more again. Raised through hell and for my family I would do it again. All the drama, the sin, and the tears from my Mama while trying to raise a man. I want Success like Obama, for my Mama and kin. I want it! Not to flaunt it, just so I can say Amen. I thank GOD. I am Moses, it's like the pen is my rod. So, I can do great things with the pen in my hand. Inspire, motivate and turn your frown to a grin. Your soul will shake, so they hate when I'm tilting the pen. They say, you will go to hell if you sin. Could hell really be that bad when you have lived where I have been? So Hell doesn't faze me, so the devil can't shake me. I was born alone in this world, so no demon is going to break me. I let my writings speak for themself; I am my brother and it's like he is speaking through death. Rhythms moved in reps, line after line until I'm moving myself. To succeed, I'm my own Inspiration, Dedication. Limitations, I have none. So just believe… I am the Son, and the Son is who we need!

Pray For me

And through my success, I will bless thee.

## **Struggle Sanity**

Whatever is conceivable by the mind

It is achievable by the body, willed by the soul

And the knowledge that God got me

Confessions from my soul don't seem sincere

Often lost in this world

And it's God I don't hear

So I Live, Pray, Laugh

Will probably cry if I die, Will probably cry if I live

I'm awfully sorry for my past, even though we were just kids

Emerged in that world of gangsters, drugs and girls

Sin, death and lust

Throwaway pistols under shirts, that are never tucked

The evils in the money, reads In God We all Trust

Chasing the fast life, trying to get rich quick

I'm from that world where you will die if you ain't toting a six clip

With this, scripture tattooed on my wrist

It's something you won't get

No path is ever straight so it's likely I will slip

But the tat is for Faith

So, it's probable I won't miss, it's logical I want this

From the Father to the Son, I'm the Son and this is it

*When I first started writing, my work mainly consisted of poems for success and motivational writings. My mind at the beginning stage of my writing was focused on keeping me positive, so I could make a way, so that I could support my family even though I was only sixteen. Facing challenges every day to make a way that was safe to travel. With no role model, that would make my pursuit for happiness a legit road. They only knew what they were taught to believe. However my belief was the longevity of happiness, so I never followed suit.*

# I Digress

    I have never been in a rush to grow faster than I was supposed to. It's not my fault I am the way I am. I am a product of my environment, the stressed, blessed and violent. I'm only 20 years old, but I feel like I'm going on 40. I've been a grown man ever since I was a little man. So don't compare me, it isn't fair to who you compare me to. Because, while you all were out skating and partying, I was at home, in the basement trying to figure out how I was going to support my family. How I was going to help us stop struggling. How I was going to bless my brothers and sisters. How I was going to keep them out of jail. *How I wish I was there when they shot my brother, only 13, but I would have had their mother crying over their casket.* I found Jesus cause of them, I swear to God, I love them man. It is coping with my loss and dealing with my stress, that's why I write so much, always thinking… planning. They are my motivation, I have to be strong.

*This isn't a poem; however, these were some thoughts that were going through my head at the time. My brother Dwight was shot and killed execution style alone with his girlfriend. She survived, which was a blessing because after his funeral, we found out she was pregnant with my niece, which was also another blessing. The killing was drug related, he was selling drugs and he was killed and robbed because of that. Black male, 20 years old drug affiliated unsolved murder. His death affected me strongly and you will see as you read on, because there has not been a year since his death that I haven't written something about him. He is a significant part of the reason I am the man I am today. He is the reason I am not where he is today, he's the reason I write. Now my childhood wasn't that of an average child, my upbringing was rare. In fact I had a Psychiatrist who told me that "your childhood was horrific" and she was astonished that I was not dead or in prison. A few lines in that passage are self-explanatory, so I'm not going to beat a dead horse. However, this was my state of mind… As a child we had nothing, but each other, so if you try to take advantage of my family, you are nothing in my eyes. I will not speak to you, I will never ask you for anything and you should never expect anything from me. Life's too short to hold grudges, so I don't.*

*I just rather not affiliate with those who've done me wrong.*

# Genesis

A young fascination with thugs and guns

The lifestyle was fun

No food where I lived, I had to get me some

Always had guts, but in a sense I was nuts

Because I did a lot of stuff that makes me sick to my gut

That I dare not reveal, as a misguided youth I used to steal

And didn't care, because my struggle was real

Marijuana and crack pipes were found where I lived

Want to learn about drugs just come to where I live

Want to learn about sex or how to steal a bike

Or learn how to hustle on streets or use a pipe

Watch the kids at school with the perfect life

I'm only six, how do I deserve this life

I want a blessing, but the urgent type

Because at home I'm alone with no water or lights

I believe I'm grown, because when I get home I'm on my own

My father's not present and my mother's gone

Just my sisters and brothers, we watched each other

We teach each other, it's evident that we need each other

When one is going to fight we start together

Because when the sun goes down we're in the dark together

It's been a rough life, now our hearts are leather

*This book isn't fiction this is my life the best way I can tell it, in the form of art. As a child my realty was movie like. A movie that won Awards, because it made the critics shed tears. As a child, I didn't understand what my eyes were drawn to, but as a man I've grown to long for innocence as though it should be preserved. This poem "Genesis" is just the beginning of what cousin Andrea would say, my way of coping with a less than fair upbringing.*

# Drifters

My feet are tired, our stomachs vacant

No room at shelter, we can't sleep in basement

We get around, one night at this house with zero down

But some nights we just walked around until we were found

Denied places to stay by faces today

Who turn the other way when they see my face?

Its hurts to see your mother beg, with tears and dread

For a place, for you to lay your head

From people who believe what Jesus said

I'm only five, I can't comprehend, but now that I'm grown I understand

The late nights on the road with my clothes in my hands

Hand me down clothes, shoes with no sole from the second hand

It was all bought big, so I could grow up in

I can see how I'm living,

A life where you would die if you ain't sinning

We are our mother's children, father given

Four men with no vision, because our fathers missing

So no knowledge is given

Now, I live off the lessons I was given

*Drifters:* I recall as a child, my siblings and I staying at a shelter for a few days before we had to leave. I don't remember why, but I do remember that it wasn't because we had a place to live now it is because our departure brought tears to my mother. Then we were drifting again. We would end up in the living room of someone my mother would consider a friend, from the living room we would hear our mother beg and plea, for shelter for her kids, If only for a night. Now that I sit back and reflect, not knowing then but these events would shape me into self-reliant and isolated young man.

# Don't Cry

Momma, dry your eyes

I won't ask about food until it hurts inside

I know it hurts your pride, that is why you lie

But I can make it, I'll live I won't die

I see how you escape your stressing

I see you in the dark; I can sense you're fretting

Momma, I can see the pain in your eyes while you looking at me

So I smile, to give you relief

You gave your all and it's easy to see

Those nights you were gone, we were on your mind

Those nights home alone with the broken blinds

Hoping that you're safe, because we knew your grind

It's hard to say, but we're not blind and we can read the signs

But there were times when we needed our mom

A kiss or hug we be missing your love

 For my mother is unconditional love.

We love you.

*I would rather not go into details about this poem. However, I want you to read and re-read it until you understand what I am saying. I love my mother.*

# Where's My Daddy At

I saw my Daddy today, gave me five dollars, then I went on my way

Those small moments, made my day

So when I see Momma, I say

I saw my Daddy today

But there were times I couldn't find my dad

When times were real bad, moms was sad

Just wanted to see my dad, I need my dad

So I walked the streets hoping to see my dad

When he's home I'm glad he's back; Look ya'll, my Daddy's back

But then he's gone and I'm asking, where's my Daddy at

I'm up the streets at it again

Looking for my daddy, so ask his friends

He's over here with a beer in his hand

Talking, but he's drunk so I don't understand

I'm only six, so I playing in the sand

When this boy walks up with a clinched up hand

Hit me in the face, and I'm confused on what to do so I looked to you

So I look to my Daddy, I felt safe with you

But your words wasn't sober, so I didn't hit him back

I understood right then, never again would I ask, where's my Daddy at

Because now I'm a man and understand how a daddy should act

*Like most young men with my ethnicity and upbringing, I come with father issues. His lack of visibility shaped and molded us all. As a child most vividness and fondest memories consisted of time spent with my dad. He would never have to utter a word, because his presence is what I craved for, not his money. And until this day it's the same way, I have developed a skill to read silence and I know his heart is weighted by more then what I could ever bare. So in reality even though there were times that we literally had nothing. We loved and I still love him.*

# Taken

Today was the day, to end bad days

We found a place to stay, but we were taken away

The tears from my Momma, made me hate this day

My brother ran away

And my only clear memory, was we ate that day

They separated me, kept sisters together

So, I felt a lot better, since they were together

Then they took me to a pastor's home

Across the tracks, eight blocks from the streets I roamed

So, I was still at home; the only difference was I was alone

From that day forward I was always alone

Since I was seven and grown, church didn't affect me

I still robbed and fought people that tested me

Robbed people who called me friend

But since you don't know about my past you don't understand

Misguided youth stealing cards and cash, like I needed it bad

Because my momma still struggled, so I tossed her cash

Love her so much, I'll give my last

So no money for sweets, because love beats candy

So until this day, I don't eat candy.

*This poem tells us how I was taken into foster care separated from my sisters and put in the home of a pastor, his wife and two kids. How I started off and how despite being in a better living environment, I continued to live how I was before being inducted into foster care. My mentality was that I didn't have to worry about myself anymore; so my family was my main concern. So whatever I had, I would give them. I would steal and give to them. I would earn money and I would give it to them. Despite me being in a better place I felt I still had obligations. My welfare wasn't my concern; however, I was only 8, too young for jail. I couldn't understood the consequences of my actions.*

*All I knew was that we had nothing. We shared everything clothes, silverware, single bowls of food and produce. As child, if you have never had to split a single tomatoe five ways, you should be grateful. We were all we had. We didn't share because it was the nice thing to do, we did it because it was the only way that we all would have survive.*

*Above all things we shared the darkness and a child that feels at home in the darkness, doesn't fear the failures of the light.*

## Thought I Was Grown

I've never dreamt those dreams

A home with lights and water, which stayed clean

My first bed, I had clothes that fit me

Clothes with no holes and shoes that fit me

Seemed like a dream, waiting for God to hit me

Instead he kissed me, but now I have problems, because they don't get me

What do you mean bedtime, ?Miss? I'm eight

I'm not a kid, what do you mean I can't stay up late

Now I have to do schoolwork just to watch TV

Homework's for dorks, lady please, just let me be

Now I have a tutor, because I can't read

But it's too late, I failed the 3rd grade

The boy can't read and missed too many days

The next year was better never missed a day

My reading got better I even got some A's

Got my first bike and learnt to cut grass and I loved how I lived

Saw this man with two jobs went to school and had time for his kids

What do you want to eat son, I just said food in my softest voice

Made me think about my past and how I never had a choice

*Eventually, I settled in the pastor's home and I didn't realize then, but now that I look back on my days with them. I realize how they changed me. I see now how their morals and standards were instilled in me subliminally. However, my first days were a challenge since they had rules and requirements that must have been met in order for me to do what I wanted. They showed me that hard work will take you a long way and you can never have too much schooling. They are still in school today working on master degrees.*

*When I was seven or when I was put into fostercare. That's when I got my first bed. I shared a room with their son AJ, he was a teenage. We clashed at first because he was from Georgia and he didn't know about my family or brothers and how fighting was the only way respect was given in our neck of the woods. He didn't understand how I out ranked him but he was there also, so that he wouldn't get in trouble in Atlanta, so we clicked. He's my brother from another mother.*

*However, the message that I want to convey here, is that once my enviroment changed, I began to change.*

*Sidenote: He currently doing his thang as a music producer in Atlanta. Check him out at modiggidybeats.com*

# Change

They took me from the hood to another grid

No drugs just love, playing with other kids

Played at the park, with just dirt and sticks

Sleepovers and ate pizza, until we got sick

Got my first job at 11, 10 dollars an hour

I only worked an hour, but I was empowered

That money felt so much better

Wanted to work a million hours, despite the weather

First camp, first dance, first girl to hold hands

First time at the beach, first time in the sand

First time that I cried, because I was confused

I didn't know what to do; my auntie had my sisters and wants me too

Leave with them or stay here, I don't know what to choose

The Moore's fixed my heart so I was torn apart

I chose my sisters, the other voices in the dark

*Mrs. Moore, the pastor wife's mother, had a stroke. So, we packed up and moved to Summerville, South Carolina. We moved in order for her to take care of her mother. There I was a kid and I did what kids did. I went craw fishing, to camps, on field trips and I chased rabbits. I played a lot, and in general, I did a lot of kid stuff.*

*That all changed when my sisters came to visit me. Had an aunt in Indiana who had gotten custody of them and they wanted to know if I wanted to move there also. Honestly, my first thought was hell no, but our visit and my time spent with my sisters made me reconsider. First of all, I didn't know this woman. I didn't know her reasons for wanting us. It could have been to keep us together, but we've been struggling so long so why would now be the perfect time to scoop in and save the day. I'm happy now, I eat every day and the only thing I worry about is am I going to be able to finish my homework in time to watch Dragon Ball Z. However, I didn't know this woman and I wasn't about to let my sisters leave with her, without me, so I left with them.*

## My First Poem (7th Grade)

When I met you

Words could not describe your beauty

Every time I looked you up and down

I stopped on your booty

Every day I see you in class

I check you out as you pass

I joked around to make you laugh

And for you to notice me

There are all kinds of people who want for us to be

Your friends, my friends, probably even God

Go with the flow baby

You can be my Bonnie and I will be your Clyde

Minus the shooting and killing

Take you to the pool in the summer where we can be chilling

And buy you stuff like you wouldn't believe

You some jewelry and your friends some weave

Girl you look cute to me

You're adorable, almost cute as me

~~~~~~~~~~~~~~~~~~~~~~~~~~*****~~~~~~~~~~~~~~~~~~~~~~~~~

*I wrote this for my first girlfriend. Once I moved to Indiana, I was fresh meat, I guess. You can tell how I wrote this that I have come a long way with my writings over the years. We were actually learning poetry and the history of the great poets. We were given a homework assignment to make a Haiku, and it came so naturally that I never stopped writing.*

# I'm fighting Again

So I can't see my family, because I don't know how to act

And they don't know how to act, but if I defend my family, I'll get smacked

Those days were short-lived like my visits back

I watch drug deals from your porch on the stoop

Use to get money from my auntie, now she thinks we're stealing her loot

So I couldn't have cash, if I did, it was hers

You're a thief! I know about your past, you took that from my purse

That's what I'm thinking, she's thinking, when she's putting us down

How are you going to talk about my momma when she ain't around?

Now we have to beg for shoes that we needed for school

Now she's gone all night until her bets are wrong

Left alone, but it's not our first time being left alone

No calls and she didn't answer her phone

She could have been dead, we could have been dead

I guess thoughts like that never entered her head

Now I have to be the man again and I can feel the sin

Back to the days when I was stealing again

Breaking dudes at school, now the mercy's gone

Have to save up cash for the next times she's gone

I got four mouths to feed including my own

And my sisters can't cook or get along

Now I'm breaking up fights while my aunties gone…I'm my sisters' savior

No food at home…lets go ask the neighbor

Where's Miss Lee at and when she's gonna come back

She said 'she'll be back when she comes back

~~~~~~~~~~~~~~~~~~~~~~~~~~*****~~~~~~~~~~~~~~~~~~~~~~~~~~

So I moved to Indiana with my aunt and sisters and at the start everything was all good. But just like everything else in life, nothing lasts forever. Honestly, this was the hardest poem I ever wrote, there's too much to be said. So I am going to take it piece by piece and explain everything in detail. When I moved to Indiana, all my brothers and sisters were living there along with my mother. So to punish us, my aunt would deny us visits to see them. She would speak badly about them to us. Now let this be clear, these people she's insulting are my family. The people I share blood with, that I've shed tears with, the only people who truly knew my story before I wrote a book about my life.

Eventually, they all moved back to Louisiana. Then as a punishment she would hit us on the hand with a wooden spoon. I don't know if she started hitting us because they were gone, but I knew that she knew what would have happened if we would have told them. My last time getting hit was when I was fifteen. I had reached my rage limit, because I was getting hit for no reason. I held my hand out, and stared her directly in the eyes. Asking myself, do this woman know what she's about to do. She hit me three times with no reaction to punishment, so she stopped. She's the only person to ever hit me when I was that mad and not get hit back.

So since she wasn't giving us money and if we had money, we stole it from her; which is odd, because I used to do yard work for her ex-husband for five dollars an hour on my Saturdays, and apparently, that was her money too. This man would have to lie about how much he paid me in order for her to not take all of my money. So I said fuck this, and I stopped working for him since she felt entitled to everything I made.

I started making money on my own, starting with school transactions. For example, buying cell phones, knifes, watches and other mischievous things kids were fascinated with at the time. On the side, I stole money, not from her but the kids at school. I used to steal lunch cards, and then sell them back to the kids at lunch when they realized that they had lost theirs.

It was the summer of 2007, and we were planning on taking a trip to Louisiana to see my family. My aunt told my momma that if they sent some money up here for gas, she would bring us down there. So they did, they scrapped up all the money they could in order to get to see us. My aunt got the money then vanished and didn't tell us anything. She was gone for like three or four days. Meanwhile, I'm cooking and making sure my sisters ate. At one point a neighbor up the street bought us some food for me to cook. My aunt eventually showed up. Young and naïve, upon her arrival, my youngest sister asked her "when were we leaving?" We already knew the answer, but hearing it set my sister off.

We were not leaving, because my auntie took the money my mother sent to the casino and lost it all. (I faded away into my thoughts, because I knew what it took for them to get the money together in order to send it to her.) Which lead to a confrontation between my auntie and sister; which escalades in volume so much that my auntie called her daughters, who called the police, who directed my sisters and I in to my aunt van and we were drove to the child protective services. We're so confused. My sisters are crying again. They gathered us in a conference room and went around the room and asked us all where did we want to go? Meaningless input on our end because our lives were in their hands now.

They drove us to this half way home type place. It was the place where potential foster parents would come to choose the kids they wanted.

27

*I met guys who had run away so they were sent there. One kid was in a car accident with his mom and little sister, his mother died and they were waiting for a relative to come pick them up. They separated the males from the females so I only saw my sisters once or twice while we were there. We were locked in our rooms at night and we were constantly monitored, we were even march to breakfast, lunch and dinner.*

*It took a week for someone to agree to accept four teenage siblings in their home. Ms. Valarie, she is now an honorary family member and mother to lost souls. We love her!*

# Happy Birthday

What's up bro…? Yea, I made it, and I made it because…

Because your life you gave it, so I'm going to take it, flip it and make it for us

And that's what I did bro, I made it for you

Yea the money's coming real slow, but I'm making it dude

I'm trying to show you the life you never got the chance to live

So I'm living for you, you're the reason I live

It was all for you and I'm doing it still

So we not done yet, we have my life to live

And I know you were proud and you smiled when you found out

That your little brother was living for you, ready to shine until he timed out

And joined his big bro and we rapped and flowed until we rhymed out

And we laughed and we cried until we didn't care

Because you was shot

So they ran, then they dropped, all the tears we couldn't stop

So we cried,

Because I cried, so you cried, because I lived and you died

And I love you, even on my worst days

I'm never too sad to write you, Happy Birthday

Happy Birthday

*This was the first thing I ever wrote for my brother and not even close to the last, because subconsciously, I always end up talking about him in my writings for some reason. You're not dead until you're no longer a memory? So I keep him alive as much as can through my writings and this book will further solidify he short stay on this earth.*

*Dwight Lashan Taylor May 16, 1983 - August 20, 2003*

## Success

Successful people do what the unsuccessful are not willing to

Because they complain and fuss, they talk actions they never do

So my success, my situations, I don't fear them

Fear screams limitations, so I don't hear them

Because I refuse to be limited by anything other than my faith

So my success is determined by the actions I take

So I can't do half the work, half the time and expect to be great

I am limited by my mind and driven by my faith

What's more precious than time, a wealth of faith

So if I am going to have true success

I'm going to have to thank God, Thank You, I'm Blessed

*By the time I wrote this poem, my main focus in life was to become successful. I wrote to motivate myself, and eventually reciting a lot of my old work receptively. It was implanted on my brain, so random times, they would come to me.*

# Reminiscing

I sit here and watch my life flash before my eyes

How do I live my brother, when everyone die's

Reminiscing on how it used to be

Thinking about the old days, just you and me

A true brother to the end, you was there for me

That's you brother, friend…you cared for me

So I thank you for your guidance bro

I looked up to you and now I hope you know

And I hope you knew I would be where you're at, if it wasn't for you

And that's a fact, I love you dude

So I live my brother, I live for you and if I promise it's forever, it's forever true

And for your kid that you never knew, I got her, she's my heart, a part of you

I see you in her and love her and you

I reminisce because you're missed, the love is true

*This is for my brother because he died not knowing that his girlfriend was pregnant with his first child. So my niece never got the chance to meet her father, nor did her father have any knowledge of her existence. That really hurts my heart, because I'm positive that he would have never put his daughter in the situation he was in. So I'm stuck thinking what ifs, but I can't change the past, if I could I would have been there for my brother. Despite that, he's the reason I've tried to be a thug or want to join a gang. My brother was a thug and when I was younger, I wanted to be just like him. I loved how people feared him, how no one would mess with me because he was my brother. So I use to try and mimic him, play with guns and steal. One day it all changed, one of my most vivid memories. One day I went to the store, I browsed around a bit contemplating on how I was going to steal some jewelry. I was about six or seven, but in situations like these, plan and execute my movements to the letter. So precise that I got away with three times as much merchandise that I had planned. It was all jewelry, necklaces and earring…it was all fake, but I'm only six, I don't know the difference, so it's real to me. So I ran home as happy as can be, ready to show my brother the goods. My brother saw me and I'm overjoyed, smiling from ear to ear. I said, "Look what I got". He's smiling because I'm smiling; I said I stole it, with a devilish grin on my face. Then he stopped smiling, so I stopped smiling, then he dropped his head and shook it in disappointment, then said, "naw bruh, this ain't the life for you". Now I'm confused, I was thinking, I'm just trying to be like you, but I understood what he meant. I threw all my gold and silver in the trash and that was the last time I ever stole from the store; or wanted to be a thug, because my brother didn't approve. He didn't do the things he did because he love it, he did it because he felt like he had no other option, to provide for the ones that he loved.*

# Our Life

I would have took one to the head, if it saved

One less in yours that they gave you

I would of took ten to the back or five to the chest

I'm stronger than I look; yes I know I'm blessed

Sorry bro you had to go so soon

Just as night turn to the day and the sun to the moon

We are lost in this world that I call doom

So how do we shoot for the moon?

When we can't afford the ball

8 by 12 ft. rooms…feet to head, wall to wall

No money, no food, clothes molded and small

Living in a shack with holes in the floor and rats in the walls

Can't afford the O-R so we 'PO' and that's all

And that's it and nothing else

We live the life we're given and play the cards we're dealt

Life's cold and it will never melt

So when I die, it will be after my death from within myself

*Here I felt somewhat responsible for my brother's death. When he died, I cried a million tears but in the mist of that, I kept apologizing. I don't know why, but I wanted to die and take his place. This poem also gives you a brief intro of some of the living conditions that we were susceptible to as children. As a child I didn't know better, it was normal to me. The moving from place to place, home to home, it didn't bother me. I didn't care that it wasn't my job to care about these adult problems. I lived in the moment when I began to think on the life that I had lived.*

## Am I a Preacher?

Am I a preacher?
If I am, I'm the musical type
Because my rhythms are rife
Just as his words, they will change your life
I'll hit you with a litany
That rhymes that are plenty
That will change your mindset from a buggy to a Bentley
Make you feel whole in a way like you were empty
Un-truncate your life from a day into infinity
Infinity and beyond
Because you'll live while you're dead, your spirit lives on
Your soul will grow and you will go on
And be what you were destine to be
A heavenly body living spiritually
So I write myself questions that I can read
Can I touch enough souls to confine in me?
That this message in my text, from inside of me
That's meant to read and believed,
Take action and achieved
Am I a preacher?

~~~~~~~~~~~~~~~~~~~~~~~~~~~*****~~~~~~~~~~~~~~~~~~~~~~~~~~

*At one point in my life I was told by a pastor that I was going to be a preacher. His premonition has obviously not come true. However, the reaction I get from people from my writings, I am certain that I am fulfilling my calling…with my God given talent. The way my art touches people so much that they tear up or feel the emotions I was portraying, while my writings are an experience and a blessing. That is the reason I chose to touch lives through my writings.*

# Dead World

Let me tell you about the world I was conceived

Lost, pain and death like you wouldn't believe

Let me take you to world of real

Desicated and murderous, it often kills

Dead and cold, so hard to feel

Hard to see, even in the mist of the day

Dark and forbidden, so in the mist I pray

So in the mist, I search

Grounded by his words through the roots of the church

Taking action with verbs just to fix this earth

Because it's smothered in lust and sin

So we die when we trust in men

So to live you must trust in him or perish like the rest of them

So let me tell you about the world I live

Full of aches and pains and bares no pills

Or remedies to heal the ill or the dead

Except the 64 books with his words in red

*When I was younger, death seemed to intrigue me for some reason. I was fixated on it and a lot of my writings depicted it. My brother died and then my aunt was killed in a car crash not even a year later. It started to seem like the only time I ever got to see my entire family together was at a funeral. Honestly, I didn't cry at my aunt's funeral, I was out of tears. So when my grandmother died of cancer, I still wasn't able to make the appearance, which made me question everything. I began to think something was wrong with me. My brother's death took them all; I watched and felt emptiness as my family members and friends of the family ball their eyes out. The only feeling I felt was ashamed, because I couldn't cry.*

# Forgive Me

Forgive me Father, for I have sin
Strike me not for I am only man
And the sin I did, I indeed resent
So kneel and pray so that I repent
Because the spirit is strong but the body is weak
So I'm tempted by life, that's why I am the sheep
So forgive me is what I say when I pray
Forgive me for tomorrow, not only today
Because no man's perfect, not at all, in no way
Not almost or close, there's no use to even reaching
I'm confused by this world, more-so by your teachings
Baffled by the leaders and uncertain of the preachers
They seem like rappers using Jesus for features
I surrender, so teach me
How to fly and to soar, so they can't reach me
How to sow, how to grow, how to reach for the stars
How do I climb those mountains, how do I grip these bars
How do I face my storms and not get soaked
How do I love when my heart's still broke?
I'm dying for guidance, but my voice is mute
I'm sorry that I lied, I repent, I resent that I ate that fruit - Amen

# Heavenly Beauty

More precious than life you are to me

I'm bound by love, with it I'm free

How would God Himself describe such beauty?

Flawless perfection no doubt my best

He would say he shared his heart, more so than the rest

And when we locked eyes, you took mine out of my chest

A picture of perfection which words can't describe

With a voice of an angel, which bring peace to the alive

A soul lifting glare that lingered in her eyes

With wisdom far beyond her years

Life full of love, lost and tears

I felt it was my job to cease her fears

No more pain now that I am here

Couldn't describe her beauty, so all I did was stare

And believe there was a heaven and she was once there

She touched me at my nerves, so my words couldn't compare

*This was inspired by my first love, some say puppy love because we were so young…seventeen years old but this girl was my world. I've always been the lover type, because the only people that I love are family. So, if you prove yourself to be accepted in this close-knit circle, the love is real. I would have married this girl; however, her family became a major interference in our relationship. From the start there were conflicts, her older brother didn't want me dating his sister. Everyone was protective of her and only her. Nobody cared about anybody else in the family. Eventually, we got around that with her mother's approval. So from then on, I learned everything I could about this girl. We spent countless hours on the phone. I knew her past and all the conflicts and events that hurt her. I felt like it was my job to make sure she was safe and never harmed again. I knew I couldn't do that, because her family watched her 24/7, so eventually that led to us separating.*

# Dear John

Dear John
I have found, that I was confused
It was lust not love, but I feel sorry for you
Please, except my apology

This wedge has cut me deep
To where, I can't bear to even sleep
I'm so tired and often weak
I pray to God from my knees, for him to help me see

To fill a need, I've found a man
To love me here, in our home
I feel God sent him because you are gone
To ease the pain of me being here alone

At first I was drinking to fill the void
But as I thought, I wanted more
To lose myself, I wanted joy
A normal life, while you deploy

I have suffered, a great deal
But I am sorry,
And I can't help the way I feel

# Dear Jane

Dear Jane
I know love and I know lust
And I had loved; now I don't trust
Please, read between the lines

Separated from everything, I've ever known
I used your thought, to keep me home
To keep me sane, to keep me strong
I've prayed to God, to keep me alive
My only concern, is to SURVIVE

Here I've met a fear that I can only accept
Four miles from the enemy, but inches from death
Here I can't drink and I can't cope
There's times when I can't think and I lose hope

Here I can't sleep or not shake
Because I prefer, to die awake
I can't image your pain or your fear
Because your reality's a dream of everyone here

I am sorry for your suffering and lost
To have become my wife you've paid a cost
I will pray for the best for you, but I want for the worst
Nothing extreme, involving a hurst

But I hope you get to share in my reality
Of what I've seen and what I see
Even if it's only the feelings
That have made me, me

I am sorry, I can't help the way I feel
Because when we got married, we made a deal
To share in the good and the worst
To love through it all, including the hurt

# Breathe

How do I breathe when you're my all and my everything?

You're what I need and if you left, I lost everything

A sorrow so deep even in death, I'll feel the pain

A sorrow so deep, sleep and death, they feel the same

My eyes waters because my soul's in pain

He knows I hurt, God knows my pain

How do I grow when all it does is rain?

When together is love and separation is pain

How do I breathe when I'm choking on the fear?

Losing you, being apart having you not here

You're my sun, you're the reason I grow

How would I prosper, if I didn't sow?

How would I live with a heart no more?

How would I breathe if I was emotionless, dead, cold and blue?

How would I breathe if I didn't have you?

This was for my first love and this is when the relationship started to get shaky. Her younger brother got mad at her and then told their mother we were having sex. So her mother had forbidden me to come over her house ever again. I couldn't speak to her nor communicate with her daughter. Her mother use to give me the most evil looks at church, because that was the only place we could see each other…we didn't go to the same school. So we wrote notes to each other and had other people deliver them for us. Eventually, her grandmother saw how this was devastating her granddaughter, so she would let her come over to her house then invite me so we could see each other. That worked for a while, but eventually being young and bold, we decided to increase the risk. So I would take the last bus, going to her side of town and I would sneak through her window. The ironic thing is that her younger brother was the only person who knew that I was over there. So, I slept on the bed with her and when somebody would open the door without knocking, I would roll off the bed and under it. Then in the morning when her mother left, I would come out and hang with them for a while then I would leave.

# Fear None

As I walk into the shadows of death

My mind wonders, but my hearts at rest

I can feel it in my heart and chest

The knowledge that God has given me and I'm above the rest

And the valleys in the shadows are beneath me

I am the glow that they feed on, until they free me

Let thy rod and thy staff be my guide and my map

So to fear is not a thing and to believe is a fact

Evil has no control

Thy mind is the remote which controls its flow

And knowledge is the gate and these words are the key

Encrypted with faith in case they break me

So I walk and I stumble and try to stay humble

But my accents strong, so my words start to jumble

But stand strong through your trails

Because this world is foul

Because God is with you and if God is with you

Who can be against you?

*Eventually, the secrets became too overwhelming and everyone started to tattle on each other. It was resolved and I was able to see and visit my first love again. However, emotions went wild and for some reason, everyone in her family had a vendetta with me. But like I said before, I wasn't there for them. I was there for her and as long as she trusted me, I would always be there for her. But she stopped…she eventually let her family come in between us. They told her that they saw me walking across a parking lot with another girl and she believed them. She didn't believe me when I told her it wasn't me; especially when in fact, the day in question, I was in the hospital by her side. I spent two days in the hospital and didn't even shower or change clothes. I didn't have a car so I had to take the bus just to see her. So we broke up because the trust was broken and my heart was tarnished. The whole situation turned me off to her type. I love family but if your family doesn't want to see you happy then leave them.*

# Rage

My untamed rage lies dormant in my silence

Shielding this world from the ultimate violence

Created by a lifetime of pain

But suppressed by my will in an effort to keep me sane

In an effort to keep me stable

That I sustain whenever I can

Whenever I am able, but I am only a man

How far past my limit must I go?

How far must I be pushed before you know?

That my silence has a more profound meaning then humility

And the urge to let you know is killing me

It's eating at me begging to come out

And show you truly what I am about

*I have always been a calm collected and quiet individual. Somehow this trait attracts unwanted attention, the type of attention that ends in bloodshed. There have been two (2) circumstances in which I felt that I unleashed the rage. Both situations involved me in a confrontation with three guys ready to fight. In both incidents, I reacted the same way and they ended the same way. There would be one guy out of the three that pushed me so far past my limit that I was on auto-pilot. I became furious and uncontainable, I couldn't be still. I approached the three (3) who wanted to engage me in combat; they were reluctant despite their manhood being challenged by one guy in the mist of the two dozen people consisting of strangers and peers. They stood motionless and silent as I vigorously taunted and belittled them as individuals and as a group of men. Their silence and inability to articulate fueled my fury even more. They pushed me to this limit through their own actions and remarks. Now speechless and confused, all they could do was stare. I looked them in their eyes and I saw fear. They feared me. We don't fear the unknown; we fear the feeling of uncertainty. I say this because they didn't know me and they taunted me, but when I reacted they began to question their actions up to this point, uncertainty. They weren't the dept of my anger and wasn't certain that I would stop.*

# Progression

To promote the progression of the minds of our youth

Our lessons must consist of thoughts, knowledge and truth

Deep thought that engulfs our minds

Developing creativity like that of Einstein

Nicola Tesla, Imhotep, Edison

Creativity that only be considered a blessing

To be known as a genius, not only smart

We must think as beings with our minds and hearts

We must think because to think is a lost art

So let us ponder and challenge that perfect thought

To dwell in its meaning and our minds impunity

To take the awareness of its existence to another reality

To embark on a journey the expand your intellectually capacity

Fueled by our curiosity

Quest taken by Gandhi and Martin Luther King

In order to take our achievements to spectacular heights

So as to think a meaningless thought is to simple take flight

And journey to a realm of possibilities

Opening doors to multiple amounts of opportunities

That can only end in success

Because all challenges are primitive, once our mind is set

*This poem is me in one of my thinking dazes. Honestly this poem was created to help me remember the meanings to vocabulary words that I had one week for English.*

# Prayer

As I close my eyes and bow my head

I pray and kneel beside my bed that eternally I live even after I'm dead

So if tomorrow never come

I'm saved by the son

Because I passed up the drama and lived for the one

But these tears from my mom got me living by the gun

Empty visions of the millions with two or three sons

Stressing over blessings, Lord wake me when I'm done

But these questions of repetition are meant for the son

Like "Am I really living, because I'm not really having fun"

And, when is success going to find me

Pastor said I'm saved yet, I'm steady trying to find me

But my burdens never fail, like timber from a pine tree

So the question still remains Lord, Why me?

What's the cause for the tears and pain?

This stressing for a blessing is like a tumor on my brain

I feel like if I die, my death will be in vain

Can't even see past my nose, vision impaired by the rain

So I'm searching for my soul, to control my sane

But if you don't know my struggle, you can't feel my pain

## Broken Spirits

You can tell by the signs in her eyes that she's been through some things

They don't even shine any more, with that heavenly glow

You hear the pain in her voice, when she speaks you know


She was thinking wife and love, but he just liked her

Now she crying in my ear, like he never even liked her

Now I'll admit that I'm hurt

Because the tears from my momma, got me feeling for her

When her feelings were hurt


So I'm writing and thinking trying to calm her nerves

Its motivation in verbs, I'm just compiling the words

Building a dream, her self-esteem is hurt

I see the pain in her eyes; I know the feeling is worst

It's morphine to her heart, when she reading my verse

So I'm controlling her tears, when she's hearing my voice, so I speak

True words from the heart, leaves her knees ill and weak

So despite all the tears, she can still see me

Its motivation, her tears move me


But I prefer to see them not fall

It's a message in my text, I will not call

But if you hear my voice, you will comprehend

All that I'm saying you will understand

Searching for my sane, the thoughts filling in my brain

The passion that I have, you will also feel my pain


You don't have to cry, I promise it'll be alright

This pain comes and it goes like the day into the night

But keep your mind and your faith, keep believing in Christ

He's aware of the strain on your brain when he's leading your life

Just wait for the Peace and the calm that I'm seeing, alright?

## Broken Spirit II

Dry your eyes because it deludes your perception
And this pain is just a change, teaching your body a lesson
Use your mind for corrections
The only tears are for joy, let him know, count your blessings

Remind yourself that you're better than this
All the tears that you're shedding, they will never be missed
This is minor Ms. Lady, you're bigger than this

So dry your eyes, calm your mind...let live and let go
Because that next thought, could be the seed of regret you know
Keep your faith and just go with the flow
Because love don't envy, hate or hurt, it's good for your soul
But this helps you grow
This lesson that you getting is a chance to sow

A chance to lean to make clear of your dreams
You a mother, and a Queen
And this pain is not seen
So truth is, it's not a thing
It's nothing
And you're something
Let him know that you hurt, PRAY <u>and</u> show him that you love him.

*These last two poems were written for the same person, who is a female friend that was in a relationship with my home-boy. She had about eight (8) years on us, but we were young, wild and reckless. A long story short, she was a grown woman looking for more than what my home-boy was willing to give. So he led her on, hoping that eventually she would stop calling and realize that he wasn't interested anymore. This left me in a bind because she would see me and ask about him, but I couldn't say anything, but that you should talk to him yourself. I tried to get him to tell her, but he wasn't that type of person. Eventually, one night she called me crying and sobbing all up in my ear. I felt so bad for her that I wrote these poems in the mist of her emotional breakdown. I left them as a voicemail for her to listen to as she pleased.*

# FATHER

Ok so let me start with, I hope you understand

All the things that I'm saying

And fully comprehend that these events wasn't planned

And I'm sorry and it hurts me, too

And I hate to be brief or short with you

But there are things that I am doing that are just for you

Separated by lies, I'll adjust for you

Just playing my cards, before your birth, my life got hard

For what it's worth, I'll do it again including the sin and get the same old scars

I had to save what I could, so you would never starve

Working on ways, so we could live happy

And I will make it work, because I want it so badly

For my son to have everything not given to his daddy

I'm only sad that your mama know

And is coping with a smile even though she wants to frown

Because daddy's on a mission that takes me out of town

So I can't see your birth and it hurts even now

So I need you strong for your mother when your daddy's gone.

*This was just something that I wrote for a female friend of mine, despite being a very intelligent young woman; she ended up like so many females now-a-days. She led with her emotions, into a relationship where guy only thought with one thing. After we spoke*

*for the the first time in years, I realized that I contributed to her current situation.*

*After I was hurt by yet another female, her and I found eachother. We laughed, we shared and she opened my mind to things that I never thought about and she became my first of many things and I will never forget about her or stop caring for her.*

*However, neither one of us were ever vocal about how we felt about each other, and I was shipped of the Germany weeks later after we entered each others lives and that silence caused alot of tears and emotions when we finally spoke, years later.*

*She ended up trying to replace me and ended up becoming a statistic. Her words struck me at my core and it still hurts to think about it. She's so intelligent. She married and she's happy now. We don't talk anymore because we know what we were and don't want to ruin eachother current lives.*

*However, if you are reading this my Monte Carlo rider. I want you to know that you always have an ear and a shoulder here and if you're ever in need, I want you to know that I got you.*

# FATHER II

Why bother when it's going to get rough, I can't give up

Like he did us, all we have is us, we can't split up

I swear to God I'm not my father and could never give my kids up

I'm the example to my seed when he's had enough

And the man that he calls when it's bad enough

No forgiveness for the man, who don't repent

Stressing because your blessing wasn't mail sent

Or in the form that you could pay the rent

Now I have to hustle, for my seed and his mother

As long as I'm alive she'll never need another

So if I'm not present, I'll still be there

From his birth to my death, he'll know that I cared

Have love for his dad and the times that we shared

How I taught him how to fight and bout the ways of these girls

How to man up and do it, when he's really too scared

How he's braver than he thinks because he's my son

And nobody's perfect, no one not one

It's not fun, this is for my seed

Whenever you're conceived, just believe

You're my heart, and just a smaller me

And my love is a flawless fee, for you being just as your father be

You'll never see another that ain't me,

Even if your mother try and taint me

I'll be yours and you'll be mine

Not forever, Just the end of time, you are mine

---

*This is like a part two of the previous poem, but with my own personal emotions and circumstances intertwined.*

## No More

Reminiscing on the past, your smile or your laugh
All these fishes in the sea, it bound not to last
Now these fishes look at me, like a worm on a hook
I use to think of you, that part of me that you took
My heart that I gave and the part that you kept
And the feelings that I felt when you got up and left
The thoughts ludicrous, it's ridiculous
You could never be the one, you're not a part of this
That reminiscing on my past, and that shit I don't miss
It's all for the birds, female dogs, Bitch
Because I'm just loving my life, both the day and the night
No feelings of regret, No drama, No fights
And it don't get no better
Because I see you and the feelings don't exist
I don't think about the past, don't remember what I miss
And I don't think about your ass, when I'm pulling out my D***
But I embrace, I admit
That your waters seemed shallow, before I took the dip
So I really blame myself, you're not a factor in this
Just regret and a lesson, that took me on a trip
All the praying for the blessings, that could end this shit
The thoughts of the past, the feelings, the trips and the fun
The sex, the kisses that began with the tongue
They all became tumors when you left, I was wrecked
Now I can say I survived, but still wish we never met
That's why I rarely call and that's why I don't text
No More

*So Romeo (I) found love again, but it was lost before the ink on marriage certificate could dry. I thought I had found the one for me, but it turned out she wasn't mentally able to be a wife. So I got married young because I felt that I had my fun up until that point in my life. However, apparently, she wasn't done yet. So I deployed to Afghanistan in 2010 and got my first, Dear John letter. She cheated on me and before I returned home, I received a pending divorce notification. So she chose to leave me for another. She ended up pregnant and now she has a son and she's not even with the father (karma I guess).*

*She was young and I was young and I don't blame her today for her actions as a child. I understand and we're cool. I've learn to accept people, for whom they've shown me, through their actions they are.*

# What am I? (I feel like a Tool)

I feel like a tool

I am here to make your life easier
Selfless with no care about my own
I am a product and expendable
A machine for your home

I am a clock, an alarm
That you set before you drift away
To remind you of all engagements
That you committed to today

I am a cook
With no identity or known purpose
I feed the many not only your own
Without prejudice, I service

I am a dishwasher
I wash the dishes I make
I wash the dishes you make
I wash it all, your cups, your pans and your plates

I am a maid
Here to clean your clothes
To wash, set out, to hang and fold

I am the help
When you're overwhelmed by life
Here for the kids
That you keep close at night

I am a babysitter
When you want to leave
With out questions
So that you can breath

I am a brace
A support for your back
When you're holding too much weight
I've always had your back
I am a cape

I am a neglected journal
For when your friends can't speak and your cheeks are soaking
With torn pages, a broken spine
I fall apart when I'm opened

Without question I do
In order to get it done
And not wait for you
I perform

I am a thing
I can be replaced
I may do it all
But it's not mine to take

Things don't own things
They're here to be used
You might find another
But I feel like a tool

And this tool is done being used

# Venus Angel

Every little thing going to be alright
Just Pray,
Keep believing in Christ
It's your Faith that fuel the flame for your light
But I'm withdrawn and with harm
In the mist of my storms
Locked in my wrong and forced to bare arm
Searching for a queen, but I am just a pawn
No silver spoon
Even peasants have rooms
If my writings my life, then my minds my tomb
Then the tears my scars, symbolize my wombs
They're just thoughts
My writings are just a part
Meaning nothing without a heart
Meaning nothing without a soul
Without them they wouldn't glow
You wouldn't feel or comprehend, without them you wouldn't know
Without them I couldn't tell
How it made me feel, when the tears ran and fell
How my brother lost his life and my life took an L
How my brain started to swell
My verbs went to hell as my words expelled
Just lost in this life
No cross, just Christ
No mention of my wrong at the time was right
I Lost Love and Lived Life
I died twice but still fight
There's No mercy, Am I not worthy
I give when I can, but they still try and hurt me
Kill and desert me
Just let me be me, I just want peace
Just want to be free
But heart will never tell, my eyes will never leak
Around my thoughts is a shell
Only released when I speak
I just want to be...
Unleashed

*There's a Pastor Venus, who initially opened my eyes to so many things and this is a poem inspired by her. She was the one that initially encouraged me to start writing.*

# Poverty Victim

I was a victim because I was black in the south

Empty kitchens…only visions of putting food in my mouth

We were broke

Unaware, of how we were perceived

Thinking back now

Probably poor because we were in need

Rats in the walls, holes in the floor

Living a life, not knowing why I was living it for

Why was it given to me?

Praying to God we can eat, cold nights in the streets

A million tears from my mother

You see that she's stressing

From spam in a can, every meal was a blessing

And every day was a lesson

From homes in the hills, to the project section

I've lived a hard life

And have done a lot of wrong to make my life right

So many tears now I've rubbed raw my sight

I can't see no more and don't love no more

Lost the love of my life and don't trust no more

Lesson learned

Never love a \_\_\_\_\_

*As you may have realized, at this point, I haven't had a luxurious up-bringing. I've lived in run down homes, condemned by the city. Everything else in the poem is pretty much self-explanatory.*

# Crystal Clear

If I gave you my love and showed you the world
Held you through your storms to show you I cared.

How would you feel if I gave you a reason to live and a reason to fight
We share our tears through love and its warmth through the night.

And through the love you believe me because you know that I love you.
And through your eyes, I see me and know that you're loved.
And I can feel that you need me, so I put none above.

So, I'm saying it's real, so if they playing, I'll kill
I'm not saying I am, but I'm saying I will

I'm saying I would
You're my better half, so you are my good

And I am your bad
So you make me better so they better be glad

That I cuffed you up
Because alone, I'm all bad and I'll fuck them up

But ease my mind with your word and my body with your touch
And if I tell you that I love you, I'll never give up

## My Intentions

I intend to heal your heart with my remarks or words
Written verbs and slurs that make you laugh
To think about me and forget your past
To forget what you had and to see what you have
A man that understands, that he's blessed with your hand
Cause you're a rare breed,
Rare to see, like leaves in the sand
And you fit me like a hug,
So put your love in my hand, so I can show you a man
I intend to kiss you until you melt
Cherish you above yourself and touch you 'until the love is felt
Respect you…just respect yourself
I want you above the rest
I was tempted today, but it wasn't a test
Cause I only want you, chest to chest
And I know you hurt
I won't contribute to your pain
So when the feeling gets worst, don't forget my name
Don't make my chest your tissue for every issue
Every boo-boo, I will kiss
To make you happy, I intend to
Make you smile, shine and feel
And rebuild your heart that time will heal
And to dry your eyes and cease your fears
So don't forget my intentions

# I have to make it

My cheeks soggy from the tears of my past years

I miss my brother…to lose him was my last fear

Now I feel like I have to shine

Whether legit or through a life of crime

Hit a lick, hit that bitch, yo I have to grind

It's my time and the stressing got me wrecking my mind

I want what's mine

But I ain't shining at all

How do we shoot for the moon when we can't afford a ball?

Or the bullets to pull it

Yo, I'm through with the bull shit and I'm spitting that good shit

And ain't looking for pussy or a chick that's considered a hood bitch

I want success, because I'm the best at my worst

They're leaking as I'm speaking

They're weeping like it hurts

Feeling me and the chills,

Compliments my worth

Which confirm my skills

My rise from the dirt…

# Father Issues

Why bother when it's going to get rough, but I can't give up
Like he did us,
All we have is us, when death splits us up
I swear to God I'm not my father, and could never give my kids up
I'm the example to my seed when she's had enough
And the man that she calls when it's bad enough
No forgiveness for the man, who don't repent
Stressing because your blessing wasn't mail sent
Or in the form that you could pay the rent
Now I have to hustle
For my seed ask her mother
As long as I'm alive, she'll never need another
So if I'm not present, in her presence, I'll still be there
From her birth to my death, she'll know that I cared
Have love for her dad and the times that we shared
How I taught her how to fight and the ways of the world
How to man up and do it, when she's really too scared
How she's braver than he thinks, because she and I are one
And nobody's perfect, no one…not one
This is for my seed
Whenever you're conceived just believe
You're my heart, a living part of me
And my love is free
And Perfect in the eyes that can't see
You'll never see another that ain't me, Pretend to be
Your Father
My Daughter, I love you

# New Year New Sorrow

I swear my pain the vivid-est
The constant stressing over life and how I'm living it
My cup filled to the rim, but no spilling it
Overwhelmed, yes I am, but I can't lose my grip
I have a seed to feed, so she needs to eat
So she needs me more than I need to sleep
So I'm searching, lurking, trying to make it perfect
This life I brought her into, is mine but I don't love it
Because I can't treat her how I want
What's a king without a pawn?
Or a dream without a want
To remind me why I do it marks branded on my arms
And link my feelings through the lyrics
Preparing for a storm
Or a war or whatever comes first
I can explain how I feel, But I can't tell you why it hurts
Why I feel neglected to the point I want to burst
Or why I feel my blessings are suppressed with a curse
From the dirt I come, But I can't seem to overcome
The dust in my lungs from the life I'm coming from
Late nights with that knife, that made me get a gun
Made me write of nights, never seen by the sun
Through the hood, I swayed
Like Will I catch a stray on this day that God made
Or will this blade get used
And the morning bring news of the youths with the tools
That approached the wrong dude
Because this dude couldn't lose, he was hurting
Brother just murdered, now he's plotting and he's lurking
Praying for a purpose, to make it all worth it
Yeah a little nervous, but to hell with this earth shit

# Cursed from Birth

Since an adolescent, I've been stressing
Praying for a blessing
But never seen a cent
It's like I'm praying for a gift that I'll never get

I can do without a deal, but my family needs a meal
So I'm praying that my prayers, will soon be real
Pray for my safety in this life that I live
Where they hate the way we live, so I'm forced to carry steel
And maybe I'll Love, but right now I don't feel

Lost love and my brother
My mother's tears bring tears
The doubts bring fears
Uncertain of my path,
Which way do I steer

# My Struggle

Please…
Have mercy on me
I'm crying out my eyes, so I can barely even see
I'm in need
Apparently, I can't cry for my father
Because all I know is lost, so I'm chasing every dollar
Hoping that the next helps the fam get further
Because no one man, is going to prevent us from starving
I'm sorry y'all, that I can't provide like I want to
So I pray to God, because I want to
But I'm too confused and unsure in what I'm gonna do
And my life's like a hell
Everything I do is like a fight not to fail
Oh well
I guess it's all old news
Praying that my poems make a means to buy food
Praying that my kids, when they want, they will have food
Feel I'm entitled to a title, since I've lived the blues
From the age of two

I swear my life has been a nightmare
Wake up and go to sleep and the devil still right there
So much pain that my mother still tears up
My brother still tears up
But now I'm on pills to ensure I don't give up

I want it all but all at what cost
My brother took an L, now I'm dealing with his loss
Other brother in a cell, because it cost to be a boss
Tossing pennies in a well, to wish upon a star
Evicted from our home, now we're dreaming from a car
On a quest for something better
Then kicked from the shelter
Now that's a fucking stain, even rain can't weather
The strain came then but the change came later
In the form of depression
Anger and aggression
My entire life has been a lesson, on how to pray for a blessing

# Am I still me

This casket for my soul
Another ache another nail
Just asking if you know
Is this life or is it hell

Are we living, ask the children
Are they really having fun
Are they smiling for no reason?
Have they ever met the sun?

Does all pain come with a purpose?
A lesson to be learnt
The aching becomes a carcass
On my soul, where it is burnt

Unable to forget
I hope and pray I can accept
That when I cycle through this
There's still some me left

# So Perfect

Picture this, a world so perfect
Everything you dreamt, just because you deserve it
Pray every day, for the life of your kid
Pray they live the life you never got to live
A house with a yard, a door with a screen
A yard with a fence, with a view that's serene
Locked hands with a man, a man who shares his air with you
A man that cares, he shares, he's there for you
He's never far from you
Your tears, tear's his heart in two
He share's your pain, his hearts with you
And he awakes everyday just to see you through
The day you were blessed with
When the stress and the rest get hectic
And the world's your issue
He's your ear, your friend your tissue
He the man that gets you
He understand where you stand and what you've been through
And still will stand as friend, if you were to end to
Cause to you, true love never been true
So he console and hug cause he loves you

# Lust

Its straight sex, with a teaspoon of love
Because we spoon then love
I love her curves
Love her words and how she pronounce her verbs
She's complex, but I'm about my knowledge
Love rough sex, don't mind the bondage
She's unique, her lips soft to the kiss
Can't no other feeling feel righter than this
And with this I'm whip
Thinking about my loss when I leave her
Even when she's present, I need her
Finding for my breath like I breathe her
I will admit I miss some things
Like the feeling when I'm deep and she began to scream
The way she throw it back, the look back
Yeah, I like that, I really love that

*****

*This is a just a random peom from a wilder phase of my life..*

# A Love Like

You will never love yourself
As much as I do
Despite me, hating some of the things you do
I'm compelled to say I love you
But I grow weary in this life
With sights to love and hold you
So I write, recite, rewrite
To make my goals true
Announcements that I've found you
Confirms that the love is true
And the absence of the news
Will take my sun and leave the blue
The pain and the strain
Your absence leave stains
On the pane of the window
Where we sat and watched the rain
And we shared a perfect love
The perfect picture in the frame
Where we lusted and we loved
Until our thoughts were the same
First we shared souls, then a heart
Now a name
Stopped the tears
Sealed the leaks
Built a family, now complete

# Happy Anniversary

Each year, on this day
I fall in love again
Lured by your lure
To lust, to sin
To go back and not subtract
Or regret a single deed
Because they brought me you
And you to me
When separated by space
And you're away from me
It gets harder to breath
Therefore, you are a need
The light in my life
On them nights when it's hard to see
The wrong from the right
You're whats right with me
And I truly do
Appreciate and I love you too

*This is a poem that I wrote for my wife for our anniversary. At the time of me writing it, she hasn't heard it yet because our anniversary isn't for another month.*

# I Remember

I remembered hard times
With the no peace for my mind
Because my stomachs on E and my belief said grind
But Squeaky said no, so I did it from behind
But took it as a sign

Because we lived the same life
And we weren't eating
With his life at risk, his purpose for breathing
To care so much to get what we are needing

I'm soaking it all in
I have to sin, to keep living
To overcome the grim in this life that I was given
So simple in the mind but a key piece was missing

## Rest in Peace

Today, we lost an angel to God

A trail marked by tears

While we weep she sleeps, ready to greet our fears

Our lost…Their gain

Behind the gates, they cheer

Our pain now a stain that she left here

Our hearts torn apart

So sadly we depart

From the ones we loved and held our hearts

Lost love, but we continue to

Show the love that was sent from you

Our love, our dove, we love you

# Emotional Scribe

I'm the scribe, so I write
Thoughts of my life
Gave my life to my country, then betrayed by my wife

Left my vision impaired
So I stared and thought a lot
Because to see what is there, is to believe what is not

A lost soul behind eyes that only wants to cry
Suicide at start, but those thoughts began to die
As my heart began to thaw and my eyes began to dry

I should learn from these lessons
They are blessings in disguise
Just messages from God that he's still on my side

I'm not alone
But I'm grown and it feels that way
Haunted by the thoughts that were conceived that day

When those slugs went hot
They took my brother away
Gripping tears from my mother had me dying to save
The life of my brother that was taken away

## The Thought of You

Your smile, your love

Say I pray for your touch

We kiss, your lips, when you're picturing us

Forget the past and what you had

And just trust

That my all is enough

So much that you blush when you thinking of us

Feeling the love, that they're assuming is lust

Understand, it wasn't planned

You motivated this pen

To write notes for your hand

With the hope that your heart

Is not too cold to understand

Hoping that is likes what it hears

And will to take a chance

Against all your past fears

Can I be your man

# Unappreciated

Unappreciated
I've made attempts
Shown love, my life I gave it
But in the end I feel, unappreciated

I've sacrificed wants for smiles
When I wanted to cry
Traveled miles to dry eyes
That wanted to die
Your sight I saved it
But in the end I feel, unappreciated

I've took chances on life
To make ours right
Spending time in my mind
Because I rather not fight
I rather rhythm and rewind
The events of my life
But these feelings, have me naked
Because in the end I feel, unappreciated

My efforts over looked
It can't be seen that I try
But don't regret my last thoughts
When I thought I would die
Your smile our love, I embraced it
Even though I feel, unappreciated

# How to be a Father

How do I be
A father to my daughter
With No example, role model

Acting just the opposite
Of what I've grown to know
Show her that I love her
Never leave or let her go
Praying that my pains
A part of me she'll never know

Inherent genes, single genes
Never seen, I'll never show
Only dreams and self-esteem
That only builds hope

That only builds her
Emitting love and how I feel
That only fills her
I will show her how it's shown
And how to know when it's real
Or when it's just words

I will treat her like a queen
So she knows what she deserves

*First time father, these are the concerns brought up by the thoughts of how would I do it.*

## Sleeping Demons

Paralyzed, with wide eyes
I'm terrorized by this demon on my chest
It has me screaming, praying for some help
But I can't even fix my breath
So I'm just thinking to myself
I'm alone

Compiled my thoughts with all my lost
And I'm approaching a vivid end
The constant stressing has me drinking
The drinking then leads to sin
Which eventually leads to night,
Where I can't clearly understand

I'm given pills to make me feel
Make me sleep, but if I miss they will make me kill
Unaware of how I live
I'm taking chances with a life
That's not mine to even give
I've been scarred to the point
Where noises give me chills

Crowds make me nervous
I blackout when I fear
The lashes from this world
Has me rhyming all my tears
Signing all my worries
To keep my pain near

*Once I arrived to Germany, 7 months after Afghanistan, my reckless ways and activities slowed down drastically. So much to the point I started realized I've only been sleeping an average of 3 hours a night since I had returned from Afghanistan, July 2011. Not being able to mask my symptoms with drinking, partying and females. They hit me all at once. I began to see therapist and psychologist and psychiatrist weekly, which basically meant let's talk about your life then I will prescribe you some pills that should help you. If those don't work come back and I will prescribe you some more. If those don't either come back and we'll find something that will fix you.*

*I began to see and hear things that weren't there. After doing some research it was identified as sleep paralysis. This is the worst experience of my life. Far worst then Afghanistan and all the lost I have had to overcome. The fear, the helpless made me determine to never sleep again. I became easily startled and unintentional touching increase my heart rate.*

# Prayer of the Lost

As I close my eyes, and bow my head
I kneel and pray beside my bed
That eternally, I live
Once its announced I'm dead
So if tomorrow never came
There would be no pain
Just open gates,
where the angels sang
Where faith isn't faith
Where you feel no pain
I pray for the day
In the mist of my nights
Where unforeseen things have obscured my sights
Have lured my heart
In my search for the light
I pray to be blessed
On top of my stress
Until the return of the sun
Where the hours not set
Unknown but certain
The subject that's stress
When your faiths believable
Success is feasible
So bless me, while I bless your people

# Another Lost Soul

I've always thought
If I don't dwell on a thought then it don't exist
But I get constant reminders, in the forms of pics
To the point I want to vomit and my stomachs sick

So I turn up to turn down, my emotional state
Numb the pain until I'm lame and I can't even taste
That I've been served enough lost to survive on hate

So I write instead of pray
Because the pains the same
We just spoke last night, did you forget my name
I am the guy who sees people, to measure my sane

Lucid thoughts of homicide
When I'm thinking too much and my actions collide

A temper shorter than an ad
I show signs when I am mad
I shake until, I'm heated and I only see the past
And you only see me, no good all bad

~~~~~~~~~~~~~~~~~~~~~~~~~~\*\*\*\*\*~~~~~~~~~~~~~~~~~~~~~~~~~~

*The poems was wrote for my decease grandmother, who past away from cancer.*

# I'm Still Dreaming

I'm still dreaming
Praying for its ending
To never sleep again
The only message worth sending

To rest is to conform
To the cells of the world
Dormant through the torment
Just a shell of ourselves

Our thoughts remain sleep
We're restrained when they leak
To refuse, to never follow
The world as its sheep

Illumination
I am awake and never taken
By the lies that I'm fed
Information not taken
Realize I'm dead to the notion of hating
For the people, I dread

# A Man's Pride

I'm supposed to provide
But I am weak in my stride
Amidst the leaks in my eyes
Take my grievances up with God

As my beliefs reach, subsides
And the speaks from the sides
Ends with the speech
Of oh. "Why My God"

I am challenged by the pain
To prove a point in his name
But I'm fighting for vision unseen
Like him, it's the same

## Reliving The Past

Please
Let there be reason for this pain
Like the purpose of recognition
To be given a name
My mood has improved
But I ain't feeling the gain
But losing screws over news
That's not news to the brain
It's the same, it never change
Like the news of the rain
I just remind myself, it's the hand I'm dealt
And a heart this cold, takes time to melt
For when this life gets harder, and I can't find my help
I have to love my daughter, just to find myself
Coinciding minds build shrines
On the highest shelf
Don't taint my shine, don't steal my wealth
I have a daughter to feed
Before I feed myself
Just let me be me
And succeed, while I be myself

# Resolution

This past year
I had vision, I don't fear no more
No more missing, just incisions on a mind tore
contemplating, the thinking that expands my mind more
Now I'm thinking and fiening for an encore
I want more, of what was destine to me
And send the problems of my past that was messing with me
I see the light, meditated now my mind complete
No limits and the blind will see
That reality's a dream and your thoughts are the beings
That shapes reality in the shape that was seen
Because every things conception was of the product of a dream
so believe and manifest what's perceived in your dreams
So what's next? New Year's Resolution.
Desire plus faith times execution
Equals success because you're blessed and believe in what you're doing

# Hush Little Dove

All for you my little dove
I will teach you how to love
Hush little baby don't you cry
All for you here's a lullaby
Un-tuck your chin dry your eyes, baby do your best
As you slowly rock against my chest
In my arms I will keep you warm
I will be your calm
The eye of your storm as I rock you gently in my arms
Side to side until there no more tears
No more pain and no more fears
You're not alone cause daddy's here
And if I have to leave it's all for you
It's to make a way for me and you
Cause it's my job to provide for you
I'm so glad and proud of you
You're my world and angel too,
So everything I do is all for you
So where would I be if not you
Close your eyes, sleep through the wind
And I'll still be here when they open again

~~~~~~~~~~~~~~~~~~~~~~~~~~*****~~~~~~~~~~~~~~~~~~~~~~~~~~
*I wrote this for my daughter as a lullaby when she was a new born.*

## These Tears

These Tears
Seem to stem from a pain
Where we craved for a meal
Just to nourish our frames

These Tears
Seem to stem from a loss
Hearts full of love
We were nailed to a cross

These Tears
Seem to stem from neglecting
Treated like the help
We were less than perfection

These Tears
Seem to come with the seasons
Reassuring that we're not equal
But with valid a reason

# Visions

I am
Visibly stressing over blessings
Over blessings I am yet to see
They say I'm gifted
But I'm missing, what was sent to me
All I know is grief
So I'm in disbelief
But to insure my kids eats
I will never cease
Through the tolls on this road
To a better me
This worn soul grows old
To achieve such a feat,
So vast, the need to eat will cease to be
Where poverty is missing me
I can see where I am meant to be
Through these visions
Where I'm living, dreaming my reality
But to dream is not enough
The thinking have me stressing
To the point of giving up
There's something missing
I'm not getting what I'm picking up
I'm losing time with my kids
Trying to get a buck
A weight on my heart
I only want for us

## She Was Beautiful

She was beautiful
But not in a lustful fashion
She was perfect
In her thoughts and actions
Her intelligence, rare
She was beautiful
And you felt it in her stare

But she was lost
And it hurt my heart that she couldn't see
How her self-woes
Took a toll on me

Cause she was perfect
In every sense of the word
Not a fault or a flaw
From her heart to her curves

She was beautiful
But never believed the mirror
Or the sun
And how it brightened to be near her

I am beautiful
You are so repeat it
I am beautiful
Repeat until you believe it
Then know that you are beautiful!

*This poem was inspired by a friend of mine, along with other females in my life that were not able to see how beautiful they truly are.*

# She was there

She was there
When I was crying and confused
To show that she care
She consoled the misused

In the desert
When I was left by love
She was there
To keep me above

We spoke of life
We spoke of the past
We spoke so long
That I forgot the bad

I forgot the reasons
That moved my tears
But she was there
And I was here

She was the light
On my darkest days
That helped my sight
Adjust to the haze

She was there

~~~~~~~~~~~~~~~~~~~~~~~~~~~\*\*\*\*~~~~~~~~~~~~~~~~~~~~~~~~~

*This poem was aspired by my friend J.D, when I was going through my issues in Afghanistan. She was the one I poured my heart out to and she helped me get over the things that were hurting me.*

# Last Love

I wrote letter to my last love
I call her sleep because I was dreaming when we made love
It wasn't real, it was make-believe, made up

Now they sleeping on me, like the D was good
They're hating, taken by what I was making good
The bad, the problems that I had
With the absence of my dad

With no vivid role model, how's a boy to be a father
A papa to his daughter, when he's never known a father
He meditates to state where he can't give a fuck
Because I love her like my last slice, I'll never give her up

This my last life, but that's the G in me
Can't listen to the media, because they the enemy
They want my baby to be a thot and me a memory
Because if you're only fed fear and negativity
You will fear to be anything that you never see

Now let that sink in
I have a skill they say I'm blessed with
But I don't preach what they preach, I get rejected
But fuck the fans who follow fools for they're possessions
When all the fools really want is acceptance

Because I was born the shit, so I'm the opposite
Don't accept me,
I don't give a shit, it won't affect me

I was born from the dirt, the dirty
The dusk in my lungs
I have a way with these word, they say he sly with the tongue
I should write a book and make them read instead of listening to me
Expand their mind, because they're blind if they're thinking they're free

# I Survived (The War on Cancer)

As I sit and reminisce
On my share of lost lives
Souls forever missed
My eyes will never dry

I am haunted
And controlled by a veer
A life I never wanted
Seemed to just appear

I fought the enemy in their country
Now my war is here
Every state's another battle
But with my brothers I don't fear

We've lost too much of ourselves
And the person we use to be
To ever turn and run
Or turn the other cheek

I've survived 1000 deaths
Both foreign and domestic
But this internal one, is a mission
With only one objective

Survive!!

*This poem was written for a friend of mine Tony, a veteran who has survived multiple tours in Iraq and Afghanistan. A man that was raised on the Southside of Chicago, found out a few months ago, that GOD wanted to see how tough he really is, so now he is recovering from Chemo.*

# My Awakening

It's been a while since we've last spoke
So let me update you dudes to some new quotes
New verbs, those words that'll make you choke
If your brain isn't big enough to see the hope
We're all missing folks
We're all grinding and climbing to different stroke

New positions, new soles
So when we're slipping, we're not headed down the same roads
I lost my brother to the same road
That I use to stroll, no legos
They're building blocks with fitted shots, where city cops don't go
And there we go, still paying the same tolls
I guessing death is how games goes

But I have a daughter, I can't play no more
I'm sending souls to those gates, who try and take her take
I want my take, my break my piece of the pie
Who am I,
Just a guy who mind is on the rise
I rhythm to give sight to minds that can't fly

Those living the blues, making the news they choose to get high
Can't envision or dream the things they've never seen
No hope, they fien and dream of broke thing
The BET fiens, enslaved by things fiens

I'm hoping that I'm potent enough to make you dream
And think on your own, about the text in the songs
Why are we killing our own?
While at war with nations that are killing us too
Now I'm praying for patients but can see that we're through

Wake up; wake up here's your cup of folgers
If Jesus was a Jew and wore dreads to his shoulders
Then them chains on your brain wasn't meant to hold ya
But to make you stronger

*My Awakening: Is a poem where I started paying more attention to my reality and the world as a whole. I became more aware of things and they started to annoy me to the point where I started writing about the things I was feeling and seeing. I began to question everything that I was brought up to believe. The absence of the whole truth is still a whole lie. As I researched and learnt about the things that I was never taught in school or at home. I began to understand that deception is a form of control and it is the reason for the current living conditions of the people I grew up around.*

# I'm Still Waking Up

I can only see 100ft, No more beyond these beams
My idle hand shaking, scraping, trying to create these dreams
The vivid picture

I got the stamps that won't deliver
But can send them first class, with some pressure on a trigger
I bet that, will make them hear me
Speaking in a language that they understand clearly
And with that, I make them feel me
But really, really fear me

Because I swear I've paid my tolls
Since a youth but this gets old
So submitted in every note I wrote, is how I miss my bro
And its hope on top of hope
But I drop what I can't hold, so I don't know what I don't know
But I hope you really know,
That I'm a problem
And so fluent in the bottom, that I'm taking pills to hide them

But the ain't working like the use to, no dude
More stress, new blues baby need some new shoes
Now I'm awake, I'm seeing that they use you
Manipulation, have you hating what's new to you
It's called persuasions; they ain't suggesting that you know the truth
Knowing that you never think, hoping that you never do

That's why, thinking will never trend
Because you won't fit in, if it do
We are men, this is sin our fruit
Why we sin, repent, do it again take two
Because we're lost

Lost without a thought, with hearts that don't smile
Went from gold around our domes, to golds in our mouths
Can't eat, can't sleep so we're grunting to a beat
Ain't trying to do no better, we're content with being sheep

# I Can See

Now as I sit adjacent from the statements that I'm making
I'm hoping new lungs, expunge the new Satan
Preaching devilish deeds
On beats, you never will read
I read, reread and see the need for he

I don't adhere to hating,
Or debating politics just simply stating
I yearn to give back, they turn and still act, forsaken
But never taken, I'm hoping I'm making statements
That making minds that thinking making rhythm of hating, is making them shine

I forfeit the bullshit they sending us and giving us time
Life without bail,
In cells, sharing squares with males that can't tell
Its inception
A peril within a peril
We're fish in a barrel, they're nuts in a shell
A cell within a hell, is a hell within a hell
So I tend to share tales of males that do care
Males that pop guns, to shield their love ones

So until we rise, I will never subside
Your free will was a gift from the main God
Not to be illegalized by a man that can still die

# Consciousism (We Weren't Christians)

We Weren't Christians
When we built the wonders that are admire today
We were salvages
On the verge of extinction, thanks to them we are alive today

We Weren't Christians
When we were sold to our enemies by hands the same color of our own
We are the forsaken, the outsiders
With no land to call home

We Weren't Christians
When they exploited our labor
Offering salvation or crucifixion
A death like their savior

We Weren't Christians
When we inspired Picasso and other renowned artist
Though our life seem simple
Our skin was the hardest

We Weren't Christians
When we fought to end our wars
But we were Christians
When we went to fight yours

We Weren't Christians
When we marched for equality
For all humans
But the law illegalized our vitality

We Weren't Christian
But now we are
So were we wrong and were they right
Because we were black
And they were white

## They hear but don't listen

I've written notes to the hearts and notes to the souls
I've had nights so bright that still ended in woes
Some like what I write but still don't know
They hear but don't listen

They hear but don't listen
But in here, I know living
No price for my sights, I'm sincerely giving
Insight's on a life, that you deserve but missing
But you hear but don't listen

They hear but don't listen
Fed lies and despised and angered by fiction
Since when did progress, imprison the victims
They're mad but can't see that the reason is missing
Because they can hear but don't listen

They just can't see
Why they are what they are
Why are the drugs next door?
But education so far
It's the system, that have them hearing but can't listen
But I see like another sight was given

*Remember I chose you. In the beginning, I left my world and chose to join you in yours, even though you had your issues; I chose to be there with you. I didn't run, I didn't choose anyone else with lesser issues over you. You are and were always my first choice. I wasn't a doctor, therapist or a big talker. The plan was to be with you through all your storms, make you smile and be the constant light of love in your life. Despite your trips to the past and memory lane for people that left, I've chose YOU! You weren't the happiest or in the best mental condition when I found you. But I stayed, I loved, and you got better. Then you fell and yet I stayed, I loved, and things got better. Then you fell again, and I started thinking, I have always chose you because you were my first choice but would you have chosen me if you had "other" options. So, it has been harder for me to lift you up this last time because I fell also. It's hard to lift someone while trying to lift yourself, even though you've pushed farther than anyone that I have ever met, even though you tend to shut me out. When we first got to Germany, we were shaky. You said you needed more help me to clean, cook, and help more with the kids to help you because of your work schedule. It took me a while, but I am the man you wanted me to be when we first got here, with some exceptions. For 4 years I've weathered your storms. I am not the most perfect or best husband in the world. But I know I am far from the worst. Everyone wants the beautiful woman, that's smiling and tossing her hair in all here photos. I chose the one that was uncertain of here beauty and didn't like taking photos because her past, pain and depression. I showed how beautiful she was I made her smile, I loved her, and her photos showed it. So, remember, I CHOSE YOU!!*

## Have You Ever

Have you ever lived a life
Where you were certain you were cursed
No more days just nights
And shadows full of the hurt

Figures in the distant, further than the sun
They twinkled like stars
I reached and got burn
This pain become scars

But these nights are so cold
I am chasing another light
Of course I learned my lesson
But the next one might be right

Have you ever

Have you ever bathed in ice or grabbed hot steel
Because you were so numb
All you wanted to do was feel

You crave to feel anything
Even if it's pain, doesn't matter if it's real
It's a reminder to the brain
There's warmth in this life, even when it's still

Especially when it's cold
You just alone with your soul
Oh how these tales get old
When you're repeating past woes

Have you ever
Have you ever loved?
Like that of a story

Sunshine and doves,
Purpose and glory

Only to find out, that there are unknown authors
That's editing your chapters
So your life gets harder
They're replacing what matters

This book becomes a cover
A cover to be judged,
Hard from the pain with in
By lovers that indulged
But forgot what love
Until it was, The end

~~~~~~~~~~~~~~~~~~~~~~~~~~\*\*\*\*\*~~~~~~~~~~~~~~~~~~~~~~~~~

*Once again I'm emotional, so I am writing to keep the thoughts from racing in my head. This is one of the most current poems in this book that relates to my present day reality. The others all have the same vibe ; if you really read them then you will know what I am currently going through. Despite all my attempts to be the perfect man for an imperfect woman, we can no longer move forward together. I'm not perfect by no means, but she doesn't deserve me, and I don't deserve her.*

## **Don't look back**

Don't look back
You're not going that way
Put on an act
Until its real, starring the play

Don't break, stay intact
You have your own spine
You have your own back
And that has been true for a long time
Let's not forget the facts

People, they come and they go
Just as the seasons
There's a time to harvest, grow and sow
Just trust there's a reason
And in time you'll know

But don't look back
You might miss someone that deserves you
And is hoping that
They get the chance to love you

## You don't know

You only see what I want you see
The strong man with the plan
You don't see what's adjacent to me
The misunderstood, understand

You don't see the tears that I've shed
Or the fight from within
The damage to my head
Because I trusted and let in

You don't know why I am what I am
Why I do what I do
Why I say what I say
When I'm speaking to you

You don't know
So don't pretend
I am the enigma
Lost from within

I am the product
Of the pain and the tears
Built with red eyes and odd cuts
In prison that rain fears

## Lie to me

Lie to me
Tell me it's forever
Tell me that it's mine
And it doesn't get any better
Than when I'm rubbing on your spine

Tell me that you want me
When you really have to leave
Tell me when you're lonely
It's only me that you need

Lie to me
Tell me that it's yours
And you need me every night
Tell me when you're bored
You think of me and it feels right

Tell me that you love me
And with me you feel blessed
Tell me while you rub me
With your head upon my chest

Lie to me
Tell me it's alright
Tell me that it's real
And you need me in your life
Cause you love the way we feel

Lie to me
Like I'll believe anything
To cease all my fears
Tell me every and anything
Everything I want to hear

Lie to me

## Dreaming of Tomorrow

I dreamt you hated me
Shamed me in a crowd
Drew blood degraded me
As your rants got loud

Dumbfounded I couldn't speak
I was shaken by your words
Every adjective made me weak
Hate and leave were my verbs

Find another soul
One deserving of my heat
For when her day takes its toll
She needs me to rub her feet

We spoke passion in the air
She shared I shared, the time was near
The attraction was there
She cared I cared, where do we go from here

A missed kiss is reminiscent upon
So I reached for her neck with hope
That she wouldn't pull back my kiss or my arm
Then I awoke

# Tempted (But I remember)

I'm tempted
To care to hug to kiss
I'm tempted
To share to love to reminisce

But I remember
Your tales and deceit
And I remember
My ails, my tears, I still weep

I'm tempted
To hold to caress and confide
I'm tempted
To console to finesse but you lied

And I remember
Every lie you ever spoke
And I remember
The death of all my hope

I'm tempted but I remember
And often pray that I forget
I'm tempted but I remember
Until the day you aren't missed

*The one thing that I am a hundred percent sure of, about my wife. Is that I can't trust her, and she can't trust herself. There is a major flaw in your character, when your loyalty is dictated by opportunity and she has consistently shown me that she is flawed. She also acts of emotion, so her plans tend to fall apart because they were never thought out using logic and reason. With her seemly constantly going through things I wanted to be there for her, but I had to remind myself, that she ultimately brought it all upon herself. No one physically made her do anything that has overall contributed to her unhappiness. She's a victim of young ignorance but she wears it as though it gives her immunity from all actions as an adult. I wanted to help but you can't help someone that would convince you to apologize to them, for them hurting you.*

## Drink Up

I can't sleep,
All I do is think
Pictures make me weep,
Here's another drink

Forget it all
How to love, how to care, how to walk
I should crawl

I should have left
And it irks me
Was I a fool, is it news
Did you deserve me ?

I don't know
Love is my fuel and empty most days
Just a little helps I go
Now I'm chasing most strays

Is it the liquor or her curves ?
That I'm chasing
But I see love in her words
Another picture that I'm making

I know it's because I'm hurt
That she's perfect in my eyes
But for what this liquor is worth
I'm paying for these lies

# The Brain vs The Heart
(I told you to leave)

I told you to leave
You're too emotionally attached
I am logic, you never listen to me
Therefore I harbor the facts

I read the signs
And I never forgot
You must be blind
Because she's wrong for the spot

I understand but know it's real
We are meant be
I can't help how I feel
So I don't need to see

She's not meant for us
Must we constantly reprise ?
All the deeds of mistrust
And damage done by lies

I can't give up
Her warmth, her touch her smell
So you listen up
We've been through too much to end in ale

Are you dumb as well?
How are we related?
The constant thoughts are hell
And need not be debated

We've been constantly hurt
Following your lead
Not this time it won't work
You're leaving with me

# Married in the spring

Married in the spring
Divorced in the fall
She changed like the leaves
Texture, color and all

The summer brought green
More light so I could see
The wicked deeds in the dark
You wasn't right for me

Isolated in the winter
Avoiding any attempt of regression
I took love in the spring
By now I've learnt my lesson

People and the seasons
They are the same in many ways
You can't predict their nature
And nature can't be caged

Love her while you can
Let it be known that she is missed
To be replaced by another man
Is true hates first kiss

## How Much

How much loss can you fit in a life ?
There's a price
It all cost so what are you losing tonight
Are you choosing your life ?

Or are you choosing connections
A firmer heart,
Find yourself reciting deflections
From warmer hearts
Those that just want at chance to start a connection

How much pain are you willing to take ?
For a chance at love like the movies portrays
That only seems to end in, you hate
I hate, and you crying real tears in your room most days

How much and is it worth it
The checks your gut
Reminding you, that you're not perfect
The feeling of giving up
And asking if you deserved it

How much

# I'm Sorry

I'm sorry y'all
But Daddy tried, I tried my best
I been trying so long Daddy's head is now a mess
Full of flashbacks, the future and a world full of stress

I be crying at times
But y'all will never see
How this worlds so cold
Some wish to cease to be

I'm sorry but I couldn't
I tried through the lies
When I know that most wouldn't
I stayed and kept pushing

I wanted this for y'all
I wanted this for us
I wanted this for her
But it can't exist without trust

I'm sorry y'all
I was certain this was it
In the mist of my hurting
I was working to make it fit

Sorry I tried my best
The best with what I had
My upbringing with my demons
An absent mama and my dad

I'm sorry but I will never leave you
Just as you need me, I need you
The both of you
Which is why I do more than most will do
I love you two

# Love is Blinding

Love is blinding
It distorts your vision
I said I love you, she said I do too
As she cuts with precision

She said this is for us
As she glowed, and she smiled
I said this is for us
But I have nothing now

Love is blinding
It only makes you see what you feel
She's so perfect, she deserves it
But her fake smile looks real

Let's take a picture
And post it to the world
Let's make them think we're perfect
And I am the perfect girl

So that the girls all envy
And the guys want a chance
Yea I'm married, so what
If they're looking and I glance

She is a pro at how she lies
She said I love you, only you, so don't fret
As I got lost in her eyes
She tied the noose around my necks

Love is blinding
And just beyond all the lies in your face
Is the question, How could I not see this?
And the true meaning of hate

Love is blinding

## There's A Place

There's a place that's forever known as sacred ground
Where passion sleeps and loss is found
That often weeps with whaling sounds
And speaks of love, and lost renowned

There's a place that we live to share
But hold so dear to shield despair
A fragile place that often tears
And breaks for causes, unique and rare

There's a place beneath the pain
Beneath the smile that shields the rain
With emotions and feelings, that is hard to tame
In the mist of excessive lost and gain

There's a place that waits for few
That lust for love, that poets drew
That moves with the breath inside of you
Beneath my chest, a place for you

# Final Thoughts

There are moments with intense emotions becoming overwhelming and are magnified by either love or anger. In those microseconds of a minute we are instantaneously granted the power to create the words spoken in those moments. We hold the power to breathe life and create just as God has done. We as humans tend to speak death and destruction into the things we love the most. Destine to roam the earth alone; killing and tainting the different paths we cross while searching for happiness, not realizing that we kill our joy before it develops. The stress, anxiety and the thoughts you dwell on today will manifest the future you fear of tomorrow.

There are people in our society who have been given a blessing, whether financial or in stature. Although these individuals possess what many of us seek in this life, they too seek fulfillment, and many are in positions worse than ours. These individuals no longer strive for a better life, they are merely content with living the life they were given. Feeling inadequate, ambition-less and undeserving, they search for feelings through drugs and alcohol while in a state of mind where their thoughts speak louder than those who are in their company. Then follows the rage, anger the feelings of being judged…….. Don't conform to any state unless it is your end state! Keep striving to be better! Action is the only cure for conformity. Think better. Do better. Be better.

Sometimes, loss forces us to become a better version of ourselves. Not that we didn't deserve it initially, dealing with pain takes a conscious effort. All the pain that has been dished upon my reality has been a force pushing me towards something better. I don't know where I am being pushed but I know that had I not been constantly pushed, I would be nowhere near this phase of life that I am in today. I know that some people fold and fall deeper into the pain. They become victims, overwhelmed by the things that they were meant to build upon. There is always a reason but you'll never see it unless you dry you eyes long enough to see its purpose. Lifes most important lessons are learnt with tear filled eyes. Pain is a part of life but if you focus that energy on your craft or something you want, you will feel better and be better for it in the end.

At this point in life, I am at peace with everything in this book. I hold no hostility or anger towards anyone who has conbributed in creating this version of myself. I am satisfied with who I am. Whatever happened, happened and it needed to happen when it did. So, Thank You!

She was perfect in my eyes but less than deserving in her own and she acted accordingly.

# You're the Reason

You're the reason

That I sleep the days away

I know I said it's stress

But I'm depressed, let me decay

And leave you with these kids

That you raise most of the day

The urge to kill myself and leave you

Is wieghing on me mentally

They don't need me, they need you

They'll forget mom eventually

I told you from the start

That I had a broken heart from the shit done to me

I was really torn apart

With that pain still in me

I will fuck you over when I am sad

Blame yourself, you can't blame me

Because I told you about my past

And being perfect ain't me

But I paint the picture well

The perfect mother the perfect wife

So Facebook can't tell that I despise my perfect life

# Keep Dreaming

I was told I wasn't good enough

To be the man of her dreams

But she looked to past, too much

And dreamt from our screen

From the doorway of our home

She sought out "what ifs" and old connections

What if my horoscope was wrong

Yeah we did, it didn't last but maybe now he's perfection

Maybe now he won't leave me

For a chick he gets pregnant, while with me

Maybe now he needs me

Maybe now he loves me and really, really gets me

I was told I wasn't black enough

Because I didn't act like the rest did

Like all you need is a card

And you'll never get arrested

I was told but didn't believe

But that doesn't mean it didn't hurt

I was told but I had to leave

You can't blame me for knowing my own worth

Keep Dreaming

# THE END

We all know the end is just the beginning of something new. So with the end of this chapter of my life, I am ready for the worst but I anticipate the best.

To my children: My experiences are just the lessons learnt without guidance but together we can avoid most of it. Just remember, no one is perfect, not your mother nor I. You're not responsible for someone elses happiness or sadness, what they lack is not your fault or job to fix. The same thing that makes a wise man sad makes the foolish man happy beyond belief. Focus on your own happiness because you can lose yourself, attempting to make someone happy that doesn't know how to make themselves happy.

Lillyana and Eli, I love you unconditionally and without regard to myself. You are my "WHY" and I love you too much to allow for your tales to be comparable to that of my own.